The Hidden W

A Journey i

Experiences of Those on the Spectrum

this publication is strictly prohibited, and any storage of this document is not allowed unless with written permission from the publisher. All rights reserved.

The information provided herein is stated to be truthful and consistent in that any liability, in terms of inattention or otherwise, by any usage or abuse of any policies, processes, or directions contained within is the solitary and utter responsibility of the recipient reader. Under no circumstances will any legal responsibility or blame be held against the publisher for any reparation, damages, or monetary loss due to the information herein, either directly or indirectly.

SCAN ME

Want to receive exclusive updates, promotions, and bonus content related to this book and others, plus the chance to win free books? Look no further! Simply scan the QR code above and enter your email address on the landing page to join our email list.

As a member of our email list, you'll receive:

- Insider information and behind-the-scenes insights
- Special promotions and discounts on future purchases
- Early notification of future book releases

- The chance to win free books through our monthly sweepstakes

Don't wait - scan the QR code and join our email list today for your chance to win!

Table of content

Chapter 1: Introduction

Autism, also known as autism spectrum disorder (ASD), is a complex and often misunderstood condition that affects millions of people around the world. Despite significant advances in research and understanding, people with autism still face significant challenges in their daily lives, including stigma, prejudice, and a lack of resources and support.

The purpose of this book is to provide a comprehensive overview of the experiences of individuals with autism and to shed light on the various aspects of this condition that are often overlooked or misconstrued by the general public. Through a blend of personal narratives, scientific research, and historical context, this book aims to help readers understand the complexities of autism and the importance of neurodiversity.

The narrative structure of this book is comprised of six chapters, each focusing on a different aspect of the experience of autism.

Chapter 2 provides an overview of the definition and symptoms of autism, as well as a discussion of the various theories and models of this condition. Chapter 3 explores the emotional, psychological, and social impacts of autism, and highlights the challenges and barriers faced by individuals with this condition.

Chapter 4, titled "The Inner Voice," provides a unique perspective on the thoughts, feelings, and perspectives of individuals with autism. This chapter also challenges common misconceptions and stereotypes about autism and highlights the unique strengths and abilities of individuals on the spectrum.

Chapter 5, "Navigating the World with Autism," examines the various support systems and resources available to individuals with autism and the role of families, educators, and healthcare providers in supporting individuals with this condition. This chapter also explores the challenges and obstacles faced by individuals with autism in accessing these resources.

Finally, Chapter 6, "Building a More Inclusive World," overviews the various social and political movements working towards greater inclusion and acceptance of individuals with autism and discusses the strategies and tactics used by these movements, including advocacy, education, and media campaigns. This chapter also examines the progress that has been made and the work that remains to be done to create a more inclusive world for individuals with autism.

This book is written with the belief that individuals with autism are not broken, flawed, or in need of fixing. Rather, they are individuals with unique perspectives, strengths, and abilities that should be celebrated and embraced. It is our hope that this book will help to change the way that people think about autism and provide a foundation for greater understanding and acceptance of neurological diversity.

Despite significant progress in research and understanding over the past several decades, individuals with autism still face significant challenges in their daily lives. Stigma, prejudice, and a lack of resources and support can make it difficult for individuals with autism to fully participate in society and lead fulfilling lives.

However, by shining a light on the experiences of individuals with autism, this book aims to help bridge the gap between those with autism and the rest of society. By providing a comprehensive and empathetic overview of this condition, we hope to help build a more inclusive world for individuals with autism.

Chapter 1.1: Overview of the topic of autism and neurological diversity

Autism is a complex and multifaceted condition that affects millions of people around the world. Although the exact causes of autism are still not fully understood, it is widely recognized as a neurological disorder that affects the way individuals process information and interact with the world around them. Despite significant advances in research and understanding over the past several decades, individuals with autism still face significant challenges in their daily lives, including stigma, prejudice, and a lack of resources and support.

The concept of neurological diversity refers to the idea that the human brain is not a uniform entity but rather a diverse and complex system that functions in different ways for different individuals. This diversity of brain function is what makes each individual unique, and it encompasses a wide range of conditions, including autism, ADHD, dyslexia, and many others.

While individuals with autism often experience challenges in their daily lives, it is important to recognize that autism is not a deficit or a flaw. Rather, it is a different way of processing information and interacting with the world, and it should be celebrated and embraced as one of the many forms of neurological diversity.

Despite the challenges faced by individuals with autism, it is also important to recognize that this condition is associated with unique strengths and abilities. Many individuals with autism possess remarkable talents and abilities, such as exceptional memory, heightened attention to detail, and heightened senses. These strengths can be harnessed to help individuals with autism lead fulfilling lives and make valuable contributions to society.

However, despite these strengths, individuals with autism still face significant barriers in accessing the resources and support they need to reach their full potential. This includes a lack of awareness and understanding among the general public, as well as a lack of access to specialized education, healthcare, and employment opportunities.

The goal of this book is to provide a comprehensive overview of the experiences of individuals with autism and to shed light on the various aspects of this condition that are often overlooked or misconstrued by the general public. Through a blend of personal narratives, scientific research, and historical context, this book aims to help readers understand the complexities of autism and the importance of neurodiversity.

It is our hope that by providing a more nuanced and empathetic understanding of autism and neurological diversity, we can help to change the way that people think about this condition and build a more inclusive world for individuals with autism. By celebrating and embracing the unique strengths and abilities of individuals with autism, we can help to break down the barriers that prevent them from reaching their full potential and contribute to a more diverse and inclusive society.

Chapter 1.2: Explanation of the Purpose and Goal of the Book

The purpose of this book is to provide a deeper understanding of autism and the experiences of individuals on the spectrum. Through the narratives and perspectives of those who live with autism, this book aims to challenge the common misconceptions and stereotypes that persist in society and to promote greater acceptance and inclusion of those with neurological diversity.

The goal of this book is to educate and raise awareness about autism, its experiences, and the importance of understanding and supporting individuals with autism. The book will delve into the various experiences of individuals with autism, from their thoughts and feelings to the challenges and barriers they face in navigating the world. The book will also explore the various support systems and resources available to individuals with autism and the role that families, educators, and healthcare providers can play in supporting them.

This book aims to provide a comprehensive overview of autism, from its definition and symptoms to the current state of research and knowledge about the disorder. By exploring the experiences of those with autism, this book aims to challenge the prevalent misunderstandings about autism and to shed light on the strengths and abilities of individuals on the spectrum.

Moreover, this book seeks to raise awareness about the various social and political movements working towards greater inclusion and acceptance of individuals with autism. It will examine the strategies and tactics used by these movements, including advocacy, education, and media campaigns, and explore the progress that has been made and the work that remains to be done in creating a more inclusive world for individuals with autism.

The goal of this book is to provide a nuanced and empathetic understanding of autism and the experiences of those on the spectrum, while also providing practical information and guidance for families, educators, and healthcare providers. Through its focus on the human experiences of individuals with autism, this book aims to promote greater acceptance, understanding, and support for those with neurological diversity.

Chapter 1.3: Brief Overview of the Narrative Structure

The narrative structure of this book is designed to provide a comprehensive understanding of autism and the experiences of individuals on the spectrum. The book is divided into six chapters, each focusing on a different aspect of autism and the experiences of those with the disorder.

Chapter 2, "Understanding Autism," provides an overview of the definition and symptoms of autism, as well as an examination of the various theories and models of the disorder. This chapter also delves into the current state of research and knowledge about autism and its causes.

Chapter 3, "The Experience of Autism," explores the personal experiences of individuals with autism, including the emotional, psychological, and social impacts of the disorder. This chapter also presents the challenges and barriers faced by individuals with autism and the ways in which they navigate the world.

Chapter 4, "The Inner Voice," focuses on the thoughts, feelings, and perspectives of individuals with autism. This chapter challenges common misconceptions and stereotypes about autism and explores the unique strengths and abilities of those with the disorder.

Chapter 5, "Navigating the World with Autism," provides an overview of the various support systems and resources available to individuals with autism, as well as a discussion of the role of families, educators, and healthcare providers in supporting them. This chapter also examines the challenges and obstacles faced by individuals with autism in accessing these resources.

Chapter 6, "Building a More Inclusive World," explores the various social and political movements working towards greater inclusion and acceptance of individuals with autism. This chapter examines the strategies and tactics used by these movements, including advocacy, education, and media campaigns, and provides a look at the progress that has been made and the work that remains to be done.

The book's narrative structure is designed to provide a comprehensive and empathetic understanding of autism, while also offering practical information and guidance for families, educators, and healthcare providers. Through its focus on the human experiences of individuals with autism, this book aims to promote greater acceptance, understanding, and support for those with neurological diversity.

Chapter 2: Understanding Autism

Autism, also known as Autism Spectrum Disorder (ASD), is a complex and multifaceted neurological condition that affects social interaction, communication, and behavior. Although autism was first described in the 1940s, there is still much that is not known about this condition. However, recent advances in research and technology have allowed us to gain a deeper understanding of autism and the unique experiences of individuals on the spectrum.

The diagnosis of autism is based on a set of symptoms and behaviors that are observed in individuals with the condition. Common symptoms include difficulties with social interaction and communication, repetitive behaviors, and sensory sensitivities. It is important to note that the symptoms and experiences of individuals with autism can vary widely, and that autism is a spectrum disorder that affects people in different ways.

There are a number of different theories and models that attempt to explain the causes of autism. Some scientists believe that autism is caused by genetic factors, while others believe that environmental factors may play a role. However, the most widely accepted theory is that autism is a result of a complex interaction between genetic and environmental factors.

Despite the ongoing research into the causes of autism, the current state of knowledge about this condition is still limited. However, there have been significant advancements in the understanding of autism in recent years, and many researchers are working to better understand the complexities of this condition.

The experience of autism is unique to each individual, and can be shaped by a number of different factors, including age, gender, cultural background, and severity of symptoms. Many individuals with autism experience challenges in social interaction and communication, and may struggle to form meaningful relationships with others. Others may experience sensory sensitivities, such as an aversion to certain textures or sounds, that can make daily life challenging.

There is also a growing awareness of the emotional, psychological, and social impacts of autism. Many individuals with autism may experience feelings of isolation, frustration, and anxiety, as they struggle to navigate a world that is not always welcoming or accommodating of their unique needs.

In conclusion, while we have made significant strides in our understanding of autism, there is still much that is not known about this condition. However, by exploring the experiences and perspectives of individuals with autism, we can gain a deeper understanding of this complex and multifaceted condition, and work towards building a more inclusive and accepting world for those on the spectrum.

Chapter 2.1 Overview of the definition and symptoms of autism

Autism, also known as Autism Spectrum Disorder (ASD), is a complex developmental disorder that affects a person's ability to communicate, interact, and form relationships with others. Autism is a spectrum disorder, meaning that it affects individuals in different ways and to varying degrees. Despite this diversity, there are several core symptoms and characteristics that are commonly associated with autism.

The first description of autism as a distinct disorder was made in 1943 by Dr. Leo Kanner, who observed several children with similar symptoms, including difficulty with social interaction and communication, repetitive behaviors, and an intense focus on certain objects or activities. Since then, the definition and understanding of autism has evolved, and it is now classified as a neurodevelopmental disorder that affects multiple areas of a person's life.

The diagnostic criteria for autism are listed in the Diagnostic and Statistical Manual of Mental Disorders (DSM-5), which is the standard reference manual used by mental health professionals. To receive a diagnosis of autism, an individual must display persistent difficulties in two or more of the following areas: social interaction, communication, and repetitive or restrictive behaviors.

One of the most noticeable symptoms of autism is difficulty with social interaction. Individuals with autism may have difficulty understanding social cues and body language, and they may also struggle with initiating and maintaining social relationships. They may avoid eye contact, have trouble understanding sarcasm or humor, and struggle to understand the thoughts and feelings of others.

Another key symptom of autism is difficulty with communication. Some individuals with autism may have delayed speech and language development, while others may have difficulty understanding what others are saying. They may also struggle with expressing their own thoughts and feelings, leading to frustration and difficulty communicating their needs.

Repetitive or restrictive behaviors are also a common symptom of autism. These may include repetitive movements, such as hand flapping or rocking, as well as repetitive routines or rituals that must be followed in a specific order. Some individuals with autism may also have an intense focus on specific interests, such as collecting objects or memorizing trivia, and may become frustrated or upset when these routines are disrupted.

It is important to note that autism is not a mental illness, and individuals with autism do not have a choice in the way they experience the world. Instead, autism is a neurological difference that affects the way a person perceives, processes, and interacts with the world around them. With the right support and understanding, individuals with autism can lead fulfilling and meaningful lives.

While the core symptoms of autism are well-defined, the underlying causes of autism are not yet fully understood. However, research suggests that a combination of genetic and environmental factors may contribute to the development of autism. Some individuals with autism may have a genetic predisposition to the disorder, while others may have been exposed to environmental factors that triggered the symptoms.

Despite the challenges posed by autism, it is important to recognize that individuals with autism have unique strengths and abilities, and that they have much to contribute to society. With greater understanding and acceptance of autism, individuals with autism will be better able to lead fulfilling and meaningful lives, and society as a whole will be enriched by their contributions.

Chapter 2.2: Discussion of the Various Theories and Models of Autism

The field of autism research is constantly evolving, with new theories and models being developed and old ones being revised or discarded. In order to fully understand autism, it is important to have a broad understanding of the different theories and models that have been proposed over the years. In this section, we will discuss some of the most prominent theories and models of autism and what they tell us about the condition.

One of the earliest and most influential theories of autism was developed by Leo Kanner, a child psychiatrist, in 1943. Kanner proposed that autism was a result of poor mothering and an inability to form attachments with others. This theory was later discredited and is now widely regarded as inaccurate and harmful.

Another early theory of autism was proposed by Bruno Bettelheim in the 1950s and 1960s. Bettelheim suggested that autism was a result of emotional deprivation and a lack of maternal warmth. This theory was also discredited and is now seen as outdated and harmful.

In the 1960s and 1970s, the theory of autism as a neurological disorder began to gain traction. This theory was based on observations of the cognitive and behavioral differences in individuals with autism, such as difficulties with social interaction, communication, and repetitive behaviors. This theory was further developed in the 1980s and 1990s with the discovery of genetic links to autism, and has since become the dominant theory in the field of autism research.

Another theory that has gained popularity in recent years is the theory of executive dysfunction. This theory suggests that autism is a result of difficulties with executive functions, such as attention, planning, and self-regulation. This theory is based on the observation that individuals with autism often struggle with tasks that require these skills, such as problem solving and social interactions.

There are also various models that have been developed to explain the underlying causes of autism. One such model is the social interaction model, which suggests that autism is caused by a combination of biological and environmental factors that affect social development. This model proposes that difficulties with social interaction, communication, and emotional regulation are the core features of autism.

Another model is the triadic model, which suggests that autism is a result of difficulties with social interaction, social communication, and repetitive behaviors. This model proposes that these difficulties are related to each other and interact to create the unique profile of autism.

Finally, there is the theory of mind model, which suggests that autism is a result of difficulties with understanding and attributing mental states to others. This theory proposes that individuals with autism struggle with understanding the thoughts, feelings, and intentions of others, which can impact their ability to engage in social interactions and form relationships.

In conclusion, there are many theories and models of autism that have been developed over the years, each with its own strengths and weaknesses. While some of these theories have been discredited, others continue to provide valuable insights into the nature and causes of autism. As our understanding of autism continues to evolve, it is likely that new theories and models will emerge, and existing ones will be revised and refined. Regardless of the theory or model, it is clear that autism is a complex and multifaceted condition that requires a nuanced and compassionate understanding.

Chapter 2.3 Examination of the current state of research and knowledge about autism

Autism Spectrum Disorder, or simply autism, is a complex neurodevelopmental disorder that affects an individual's social interaction, communication, and behavior. The condition has been the subject of much research and study over the years, and much has been learned about the nature, causes, and manifestation of autism. However, despite the progress that has been made, there is still much that remains unknown about the disorder and how it affects those who live with it.

The current state of research and knowledge about autism is quite advanced, but it is still far from complete. Many theories and models of autism have been proposed over the years, and these have helped to shed light on various aspects of the condition. For example, one popular theory is that autism is caused by a combination of genetic and environmental factors, such as exposure to toxins or viral infections. Another theory is that autism is caused by a malfunction in the brain's neural circuitry, which leads to difficulties with social interaction, communication, and other aspects of behavior.

Despite the many theories and models that have been proposed, there is still much that remains unknown about the underlying causes of autism. For example, while it is widely accepted that genetics play a role in the development of the disorder, it is still unclear exactly how the genes interact with environmental factors to cause the symptoms of autism. Additionally, it is unclear exactly how the brain's neural circuitry is affected by autism, and how this affects behavior.

In terms of research and knowledge about the manifestation of autism, there has been much progress in recent years. For example, researchers have developed a wide range of diagnostic tools and assessments that can be used to identify individuals with autism, and to determine the severity of their symptoms. These tools include standardized tests, questionnaires, and observation-based assessments, and they have helped to improve the accuracy and reliability of autism diagnoses.

Despite the progress that has been made in terms of research and knowledge about autism, there are still many challenges that remain. For example, there is a lack of consensus about the exact definition of autism, and this can lead to difficulties in diagnosing the condition and providing appropriate treatment. Additionally, there is still a lack of understanding about the experiences of individuals with autism, and this can make it difficult for them to access the support and resources they need to live meaningful and fulfilling lives.

In conclusion, the current state of research and knowledge about autism is quite advanced, but there is still much that remains unknown. While much progress has been made in terms of understanding the causes, manifestation, and treatment of the disorder, there are still many challenges that must be addressed in order to provide better support and resources for individuals with autism. As such, it is essential that the scientific and medical communities continue to work together to further our understanding of this complex and fascinating condition.

Chapter 2.3.1: Historical Perspective of Autism Research

The history of autism research dates back to the early 20th century, when psychiatrist Leo Kanner first described the condition in 1943 as "early infantile autism." Since then, the understanding of autism has evolved and expanded, with new theories and models emerging to explain the symptoms and experiences of individuals on the autism spectrum.

In the early years of autism research, the focus was primarily on the behavior of individuals with autism, with an emphasis on their difficulties with social interaction, communication, and repetitive behaviors. This led to a view of autism as a mental illness or developmental disorder, rather than a neurodivergent condition.

In the 1970s and 1980s, research began to shift towards a biological understanding of autism, with theories focusing on the role of genetics, brain structure, and neurotransmitter imbalances in the development of autism. This was also a time of increased public awareness of autism, with advocacy organizations emerging to support individuals with autism and their families.

In the 1990s and 2000s, advances in technology and research methodologies allowed for a more comprehensive understanding of autism. The development of functional magnetic resonance imaging (fMRI) and other brain imaging techniques allowed researchers to study the brain structure and function of individuals with autism, leading to new insights into the neural basis of autism.

In 2013, the fifth edition of the Diagnostic and Statistical Manual of Mental Disorders (DSM-5) marked a significant shift in the understanding of autism, with the consolidation of previously separate diagnostic categories into a single diagnosis of autism spectrum disorder (ASD). This new understanding of autism emphasized the wide range of symptoms and abilities within the autism spectrum, rather than a single set of symptoms or behaviors.

Despite the advances in autism research over the past several decades, there is still much to be learned about the causes, experiences, and outcomes of autism. Research into the neurobiological basis of autism is ongoing, with new theories and models emerging to explain the complex interplay of genetic and environmental factors in the development of autism.

In conclusion, the history of autism research is marked by a growing understanding of the complexity and diversity of autism, as well as an ongoing effort to better understand the experiences of individuals with autism and to support them in their lives. With continued research and advocacy, we can work towards a more inclusive and accepting world for individuals on the autism spectrum.

Chapter 2.3.2 Advances in Diagnosis and Treatment of Autism

Autism, also known as Autism Spectrum Disorder (ASD), is a complex developmental disorder that affects social interaction, communication, and behavior. Over the past several decades, there have been numerous advances in the diagnosis and treatment of autism, leading to a better understanding of this disorder and the ways in which it can be addressed.

Diagnosis of Autism:

Traditionally, the diagnosis of autism was based on behavioral observation and subjective assessments, but in recent years, there has been a shift towards more objective diagnostic methods. For example, advancements in brain imaging technology have allowed researchers to study the brain activity of individuals with autism and compare it to that of neurotypical individuals, providing a more accurate and nuanced understanding of the disorder.

One of the most significant advancements in the diagnosis of autism has been the development of standardized assessment tools, such as the Autism Diagnostic Observation Schedule (ADOS) and the Autism Diagnostic Interview-Revised (ADI-R). These tools are designed to objectively measure the social and communication skills of individuals with autism, providing a more accurate and consistent diagnosis.

Treatment of Autism:

The treatment of autism has also seen significant advances over the years. In the past, individuals with autism were often subjected to institutionalization and in some cases, even subjected to cruel and inhumane treatments. Today, however, there is a greater understanding of the importance of early intervention and evidence-based treatment approaches.

One of the most well-known and effective treatments for autism is Applied Behavior

Analysis (ABA). This treatment involves working with an individual with autism on specific skills, such as social interaction, communication, and behavior, through positive reinforcement and repetition. ABA has been shown to be effective in improving the skills of individuals with autism, particularly when it is implemented at an early age.

Another promising treatment approach is Occupational Therapy (OT). This treatment involves working with individuals with autism to improve their ability to participate in daily activities, such as eating, dressing, and using the bathroom, as well as improving fine motor skills. OT has been shown to be particularly effective in addressing the sensory processing difficulties that many individuals with autism experience.

There have also been advances in the use of medication for individuals with autism. For example, the use of antipsychotic medication, such as risperidone, has been shown to be effective in reducing challenging behaviors in some individuals with autism. Additionally, the use of selective serotonin reuptake inhibitors

(SSRIs) has been shown to be effective in treating anxiety and depression in individuals with autism.

Despite these advances, it is important to note that there is no cure for autism, and the best way to address the disorder is through a combination of treatments that are tailored to the individual's specific needs. This may include a combination of therapy, medication, and support services.

Conclusion:

In conclusion, the diagnosis and treatment of autism has come a long way over the years, but there is still much work to be done. Advances in brain imaging, standardized assessment tools, and evidence-based treatment approaches have greatly improved our understanding of autism and the ways in which it can be addressed. However, it is important to remember that each individual with autism is unique and requires an individualized approach to treatment that takes into account their specific needs and strengths.

Chapter 2.3.3 The role of technology in autism research

Autism is a complex neurological disorder that affects the development of social interaction, communication, and behavior. Over the years, the field of autism research has grown significantly, and new advancements in technology have allowed researchers to better understand the underlying causes of autism and develop new diagnostic tools and treatments.

One of the key ways that technology has impacted autism research is through the use of imaging techniques. Advances in brain imaging technologies, such as magnetic resonance imaging (MRI) and functional magnetic resonance imaging (fMRI), have allowed researchers to gain a better understanding of the brain structure and function of individuals with autism. For example, studies have shown that the brains of individuals with autism are different from those without autism in terms of the size and connectivity of certain regions, including the amygdala, the temporal lobe, and the corpus callosum.

Another way technology has impacted autism research is through the use of genetic testing. Recent advancements in genetic sequencing technologies have allowed researchers to identify specific genes associated with autism and the underlying genetic mutations that contribute to the disorder. For example, studies have shown that the deletion or duplication of certain genes on chromosome 15 is associated with autism. These findings have opened up new avenues for research into the underlying causes of autism and the development of targeted treatments.

Technology has also impacted autism research through the use of wearable technology. For example, wearable devices such as smartwatches, fitness trackers, and sensors can be used to monitor the movements, physiological responses, and behavior of individuals with autism. This information can be used to help diagnose and track the progression of autism, and to develop new treatments that are tailored to the needs of each individual.

Finally, technology has also impacted autism research through the use of digital tools and platforms. For example, online resources such as social media and discussion forums allow individuals with autism and their families to connect and share their experiences and knowledge. Additionally, digital platforms such as teletherapy allow individuals with autism to access behavioral and cognitive therapies from the comfort of their own homes, even if they live in remote areas.

In conclusion, technology has played a crucial role in advancing the field of autism research and improving our understanding of the disorder. With the continued development of new technologies and tools, we can expect to see further progress in the years to come. The hope is that this progress will lead to new treatments and support systems that will improve the lives of individuals with autism and their families.

Chapter 3: The Experience of Autism

Autism is a complex and often misunderstood condition that can affect a person's ability to communicate, interact with others, and engage in everyday activities. While autism has been the subject of extensive research, the experiences of individuals with autism remain largely unknown. In this chapter, we will explore the personal experiences of individuals with autism, including the author's experiences, and examine the emotional, psychological, and social impacts of the condition.

Personal Experiences of Individuals with Autism

Living with autism can be both challenging and rewarding. For many individuals with autism, daily life is filled with struggles, such as difficulty communicating and connecting with others, sensory sensitivities, and repetitive behaviors. However, individuals with autism also experience unique joys and strengths that come from their unique perspectives and ways of thinking.

The author's experience with autism is a personal and emotional journey that has been marked by both challenges and triumphs. Growing up, the author struggled with social interaction and communication, often feeling overwhelmed and misunderstood. However, through hard work and dedication, the author has learned to embrace their autism and has found success in their personal and professional life.

The emotional and psychological impact of autism is significant for individuals with the condition. For many, the experience of being misunderstood and excluded can lead to feelings of isolation and loneliness. Additionally, individuals with autism may experience anxiety, depression, and other mental health issues related to their condition.

Challenges and Barriers Faced by Individuals with Autism

Individuals with autism face many challenges in their daily lives, including difficulty communicating and interacting with others, sensory sensitivities, and repetitive behaviors. These challenges can make it difficult for individuals with autism to participate in everyday activities and engage with their communities.

One of the most significant barriers faced by individuals with autism is the lack of understanding and acceptance from others. Stereotypes and misconceptions about autism are widespread, and individuals with autism are often marginalized and excluded from mainstream society. This exclusion can lead to feelings of isolation and loneliness, further exacerbating the challenges they already face.

Another significant barrier faced by individuals with autism is the lack of support and resources available to them. Many individuals with autism struggle to access the resources they need to thrive, such as healthcare, education, and employment. This lack of support can make it difficult for individuals with autism to reach their full potential and lead fulfilling lives.

Conclusion

The experiences of individuals with autism are unique and diverse. While living with autism can be challenging, it is also filled with unique strengths and joys. Understanding the experiences of individuals with autism and the challenges they face is essential to promoting greater understanding and acceptance of neurological diversity. Through this chapter, we hope to shed light on the personal experiences of individuals with autism and the need for a more inclusive and supportive world.

Chapter 3.1: Presentation of the Personal Experiences of Individuals with Autism, Including the Experiences of the Author

Autism is a neurodevelopmental disorder that affects millions of individuals and families around the world. Despite its prevalence, there is still much that is misunderstood about the experiences of individuals with autism. This chapter aims to shed light on the diverse and complex experiences of those on the spectrum. By sharing the stories and perspectives of individuals with autism, including the author's own experiences, this chapter aims to help readers gain a deeper understanding of the challenges and triumphs of those on the autism spectrum.

First, it is important to note that autism is a spectrum disorder, meaning that each individual with autism is unique in their own way. The experiences of those with autism can vary widely depending on their individual strengths and challenges, as well as environmental factors such as family support and access to resources. However, despite these differences, there are certain experiences that are common among individuals with autism, and these experiences are worth exploring.

One of the most notable experiences of those with autism is social difficulty. Individuals with autism may struggle with social cues, such as eye contact, body language, and conversation skills. They may also have difficulty forming and maintaining social relationships, which can lead to feelings of isolation and loneliness. The lack of social understanding and connection can also make it difficult for individuals with autism to engage in social activities, such as playdates, parties, and even school. This can result in a lack of social skills and experiences that are critical for healthy development and well-being.

Another common experience of those with autism is sensory sensitivity. Individuals with autism may have heightened or decreased sensitivity to certain sensory inputs, such as sound, light, touch, and smell. This can make everyday experiences, such as a trip to the grocery store or a visit to a friend's home, incredibly overwhelming and stressful. Sensory sensitivity can also affect sleep, causing individuals with autism to struggle with insomnia and other sleep-related issues.

The experience of autism also includes a range of cognitive and communication differences. For example, individuals with autism may have difficulty with language and communication, including both verbal and nonverbal communication. They may also struggle with executive functioning skills, such as planning, organizing, and completing tasks. This can result in difficulties in school, work, and daily life, leading to feelings of frustration and inadequacy.

It is worth noting that the experiences of individuals with autism are not all negative. Many individuals with autism possess unique strengths and abilities, such as heightened attention to detail, a love for routine, and a special interest in specific topics. For example, individuals with autism may have a remarkable ability to remember and recall information, leading to expertise in their area of interest. They may also have a deep appreciation for patterns and logic, making them valuable contributors in fields such as science, engineering, and mathematics.

The author's personal experiences with autism have been a mixture of both challenges and strengths. Growing up, the author struggled with social skills and relationships, which often resulted in feelings of loneliness and isolation. The author also struggled with sensory sensitivity, especially in noisy and overstimulating environments. However, the author's unique interests and abilities in music and science have provided a source of solace and fulfillment throughout life. The author is grateful for the support and understanding of friends and family, as well as access to resources and support systems, which have been critical in helping the author navigate the challenges of autism and thrive in life.

In conclusion, the experiences of individuals with autism are diverse, complex, and often challenging. By sharing the stories and perspectives of individuals with autism, including the author's own experiences, this chapter aims to shed light on the difficulties and triumphs that come with being on the spectrum. Through these stories, we hope to break down stereotypes and misconceptions, and offer a more nuanced understanding of what it means to be autistic. Additionally, by highlighting the challenges that individuals with autism face, we hope to raise awareness of the need for increased support and resources, both for individuals and for the families who love and care for them. Ultimately, our goal is to help create a more inclusive world that recognizes and values the unique strengths and abilities of individuals with autism, and celebrates the richness and diversity of neurological diversity.

Chapter 3.2 Exploration of the Emotional, Psychological, and Social Impacts of Autism

Autism is a neurodevelopmental disorder that affects an individual's ability to communicate, interact socially, and form relationships with others. While some individuals with autism may have average or above average intelligence, the symptoms of autism can have a profound impact on their emotional, psychological, and social well-being. This chapter explores the various emotional, psychological, and social impacts of autism and the ways in which individuals with autism navigate these challenges.

Emotional Impacts

Individuals with autism may experience a range of emotional difficulties, including anxiety, depression, and mood swings. These emotions may be related to the symptoms of autism itself, or may stem from difficulties with social interaction, bullying, and lack of support. For many individuals with autism, their experience of the world can be a confusing and overwhelming place. The social demands of school, work, and relationships can be especially difficult, leading to feelings of anxiety and stress.

In addition to these common emotional difficulties, individuals with autism may also struggle with self-esteem and self-worth. This can be due to the stigma and stereotypes surrounding autism, as well as difficulties with social interaction and communication. For example, some individuals with autism may feel isolated and alone, as they struggle to connect with others and form meaningful relationships. This can lead to feelings of low self-esteem and a sense of worthlessness.

Psychological Impacts

The psychological impacts of autism can be equally challenging. For example, individuals with autism may experience difficulties with executive function, which can impact their ability to plan, prioritize, and organize their thoughts and actions. This can make it difficult for them to complete tasks and succeed in school or work. Additionally, individuals with autism may also struggle with sensory processing difficulties, which can make everyday activities such as shopping, eating, and using public transportation overwhelming and stressful.

Social Impacts

The social impacts of autism can be far-reaching and complex. For example, individuals with autism may struggle with social interaction and communication, which can impact their ability to form relationships and make friends. This can lead to feelings of isolation and loneliness, which can in turn contribute to other emotional and psychological difficulties. Additionally, individuals with autism may also experience bullying, as they may be perceived as different or "weird" by their peers.

The lack of support and understanding in society can also contribute to the social impacts of autism. For example, some individuals with autism may struggle to find employment or housing, as they are not always able to meet the social and communication demands of these environments. This can lead to feelings of frustration, anger, and hopelessness.

In conclusion, the emotional, psychological, and social impacts of autism are far-reaching and complex. It is important for individuals with autism to receive the support and understanding they need to navigate these challenges and live full, meaningful lives. By sharing the experiences of individuals with autism, this chapter aims to shed light on the various emotional, psychological, and social impacts of autism and the need for greater understanding and acceptance of neurological diversity.

Chapter 3.3 Discussion of the Challenges and Barriers Faced by Individuals with Autism

In the previous sections, we explored the personal experiences of individuals with autism, including the emotional, psychological, and social impacts of this condition. However, the experiences of individuals with autism are not just defined by these internal factors, but also by the numerous challenges and barriers they face in the world around them. In this section, we will examine some of these challenges and barriers, and their impact on the lives of individuals with autism.

One of the biggest challenges faced by individuals with autism is the lack of understanding and acceptance from the people around them. This can lead to isolation, discrimination, and bullying, which can have a significant impact on their mental health and wellbeing. For example, a lack of understanding from teachers and classmates can result in difficulties in the educational setting, including exclusion from social activities, poor academic performance, and a negative school experience overall.

Another challenge faced by individuals with autism is the difficulty in forming and maintaining social relationships. This can be due to difficulties with communication, social skills, and the interpretation of social cues, which can result in feelings of loneliness and isolation. This can be especially challenging for individuals with autism who are looking to form romantic relationships, as they may face additional barriers in finding partners who understand and accept their condition.

The difficulty in communicating can also result in misunderstandings, which can lead to conflicts and misinterpretations of the individual's intentions and behavior. This can be particularly challenging in situations such as the workplace, where effective communication is key to success. For individuals with autism, this can result in difficulties in finding and retaining employment, which can have significant financial and personal consequences.

The healthcare system can also present barriers for individuals with autism. This can include a lack of access to specialized services and support, long wait times for appointments, and a lack of understanding and compassion from healthcare providers. For example, individuals with autism may struggle to express their needs and concerns to medical professionals, which can result in misdiagnosis or inadequate treatment. This can be especially challenging for those with co-occurring conditions, such as mental health conditions or physical disabilities.

Another challenge faced by individuals with autism is navigating the legal and criminal justice systems. For example, individuals with autism may struggle to understand their rights and responsibilities, or may be misinterpreted as non-compliant or resistant in situations involving law enforcement. This can result in negative outcomes, such as wrongful arrests or discrimination in the justice system.

In conclusion, the challenges and barriers faced by individuals with autism are many and varied, and can have a significant impact on their lives. Understanding and addressing these challenges is essential for promoting the rights and wellbeing of individuals with autism, and for creating a more inclusive and supportive world for everyone. By highlighting these challenges, this chapter aims to increase awareness and understanding of the experiences of individuals with autism, and to encourage efforts to create a more supportive and inclusive society for everyone.

Chapter 3.3.1 Navigating the School and Work Environment

For many individuals with autism, navigating the school and work environment can be a significant challenge. Despite progress in the understanding and acceptance of autism, the majority of schools and workplaces are not yet equipped to meet the unique needs of individuals on the spectrum. This can result in a range of difficulties, from difficulties in social interaction and communication, to problems with sensory processing, to difficulties with organization and time management.

One common experience for individuals with autism in school is the struggle with social interaction. Many children on the spectrum struggle with making friends and understanding social cues, which can lead to feelings of isolation and loneliness. This can be particularly challenging for those who have difficulty with verbal communication, as they may feel excluded from social activities and conversations with their peers.

In the workplace, individuals with autism may face challenges in communication, especially when it comes to collaborating with coworkers and completing tasks as part of a team. They may also have difficulties with organization and time management, which can impact their ability to meet deadlines and complete tasks efficiently. This can lead to difficulties in securing and retaining employment, as well as in reaching their full potential in their careers.

Despite these challenges, there are many individuals with autism who have been successful in school and in their careers. Some have found success by seeking out supportive environments, such as schools that specialize in teaching students with autism, or employers who are open to making accommodations for their needs. Others have developed strategies for managing their difficulties, such as using organizational tools, taking breaks to reduce stress and anxiety, or seeking out additional support from family and friends.

In conclusion, the school and work environment can be challenging for individuals with autism, but with the right support and accommodations, they can overcome these difficulties and reach their full potential. It is important for schools and employers to become more aware of the unique needs of individuals on the spectrum, and to work to create environments that are inclusive and supportive for all. By doing so, we can help to ensure that individuals with autism are able to reach their full potential and lead fulfilling and productive lives.

Chapter 3.3.2 Accessing Healthcare Services and Support

The journey towards accessing healthcare services and support for individuals with autism can be a difficult and frustrating experience. Many individuals with autism face significant barriers in accessing the care and support they need, from long wait times to limited access to specialized services.

For many individuals with autism, the process of accessing healthcare services begins with a diagnosis. However, the process of obtaining a diagnosis can be challenging in and of itself. In some cases, individuals with autism may not exhibit the symptoms that are typically associated with the disorder, making it difficult for healthcare providers to diagnose the condition. Furthermore, there often long wait times for appointments with specialists who are trained in diagnosing autism, and the cost of these appointments can be prohibitively expensive for some families.

Once an individual with autism has received a diagnosis, they may still face significant barriers in accessing the care and support they need. For many individuals with autism, there are limited options for specialized care, and many healthcare providers lack the training and expertise to address the unique needs of individuals with autism. Furthermore, there is a widespread lack of awareness about the disorder and the needs of individuals with autism, making it difficult for individuals to advocate for themselves and access the care they need.

One of the greatest challenges faced by individuals with autism when accessing healthcare services is the lack of resources and support for families. Many families struggle to find the time, resources, and support they need to help their loved one with autism access the care and support they need. Furthermore, the cost of care for individuals with autism can be prohibitively expensive, and many families are unable to afford the services and support their loved one needs.

Despite these challenges, there are many organizations and resources that are working to support individuals with autism and their families in accessing the care and support they need. From advocacy groups to specialized healthcare clinics, there is a growing movement to improve the availability and quality of care for individuals with autism. By working together and advocating for the needs of individuals with autism, we can help ensure that everyone has access to the care and support they need to lead fulfilling and productive lives.

In conclusion, the journey towards accessing healthcare services and support for individuals with autism can be a challenging and frustrating experience. However, by working together and advocating for the needs of individuals with autism, we can help ensure that everyone has access to the care and support they need to lead fulfilling and productive lives. By sharing the stories and perspectives of individuals with autism, including the author's own experiences, this chapter aims to raise awareness about the barriers faced by individuals with autism in accessing healthcare services and support and to encourage greater understanding and acceptance of neurological diversity.

Chapter 3.3.3 Overcoming Stigma and Prejudice

Stigma and prejudice are two of the biggest challenges faced by individuals with autism. Despite the fact that autism is a neurodevelopmental condition that affects millions of people around the world, it is still widely misunderstood and stigmatized. This can result in a range of negative experiences for individuals with autism, including exclusion, discrimination, and bullying.

One of the biggest contributors to the stigma surrounding autism is a lack of knowledge and understanding about the condition. Many people still associate autism with the outdated stereotype of the "Rain Man" character, who is socially awkward and intellectually gifted. This stereotype not only perpetuates misconceptions about autism but also reinforces the idea that individuals with autism are "other" and different from the rest of society.

The impact of stigma on individuals with autism can be devastating. People with autism may be excluded from social activities, isolated from their peers, and subjected to bullying and harassment. This can lead to a range of negative emotions, including anxiety, depression, and low self-esteem.

Despite these challenges, individuals with autism are speaking out about their experiences and advocating for greater understanding and acceptance. They are sharing their stories and perspectives, and working to educate others about what it is really like to live with autism. This is an important step in overcoming the stigma and prejudice that still exists around autism.

One of the ways in which individuals with autism are breaking down these barriers is by speaking out about their experiences. By sharing their stories, they are helping to humanize autism and give a voice to the millions of people who live with this condition. They are also raising awareness about the challenges that they face and the support that they need to thrive.

Another important aspect of overcoming the stigma and prejudice surrounding autism is education. By educating others about autism, individuals with autism are helping to break down the barriers that exist between themselves and the rest of society. They are also working to create a more inclusive and accepting world, where people with autism are valued and respected for who they are.

The media also has a critical role to play in overcoming the stigma and prejudice surrounding autism. By portraying individuals with autism in a positive light, the media can help to reduce the negative stereotypes that still exist and promote greater understanding and acceptance of autism. For example, shows like "Atypical" and "The Good Doctor" are helping to humanize autism and raise awareness about the experiences of individuals with autism.

In conclusion, overcoming the stigma and prejudice surrounding autism is a critical challenge for individuals with autism. By sharing their stories, advocating for greater understanding and acceptance, and working to educate others about autism, individuals with autism are helping to create a more inclusive and accepting world. Through these efforts, individuals with autism are not only breaking down the barriers that exist between themselves and the rest of society, but they are also creating a brighter future for all people with autism.

Chapter 4: The Inner Voice

For many individuals with autism, the world can be a confusing and overwhelming place, where social cues and expectations are often difficult to understand and navigate. Despite this, individuals with autism often possess unique perspectives and insights into the world, offering a valuable contribution to society. In this chapter, we explore the thoughts, feelings, and perspectives of individuals with autism, seeking to shed light on the hidden world of autism and the inner experiences of those on the spectrum.

One common misconception about autism is that individuals with autism lack empathy or the ability to understand and express emotions. However, this could not be further from the truth. Individuals with autism often experience a wide range of emotions, including joy, sadness, anger, and frustration. However, they may experience these emotions differently than neurotypical individuals, which can lead to misunderstandings and miscommunications.

For many individuals with autism, the greatest challenge they face is the difficulty in communicating their thoughts and feelings to others. This can result in feelings of loneliness, frustration, and anger, as individuals with autism struggle to be understood and heard. Despite these difficulties, many individuals with autism have found creative and innovative ways to express themselves and share their experiences with others.

One way that individuals with autism can share their inner voice is through art and writing. For example, the author of this book is an artist and writer who uses her talents to express her thoughts, feelings, and experiences with autism. By sharing her stories and perspectives, she hopes to help others better understand and appreciate the unique contributions of individuals with autism.

Another way that individuals with autism can share their inner voice is through advocacy and activism. Many individuals with autism have become passionate advocates for greater understanding, acceptance, and inclusion of individuals with autism, using their voices and experiences to educate others and bring about change. For example, many individuals with autism participate in local and national autism organizations, working together to promote understanding and acceptance of autism.

In addition to advocacy and activism, many individuals with autism also participate in self-help and support groups. These groups provide a safe and supportive environment for individuals with autism to connect with others, share their experiences, and find comfort and encouragement. By coming together with others who share similar experiences and challenges, individuals with autism can find strength and hope, and build a sense of community and belonging.

Despite the many challenges and barriers faced by individuals with autism, there are also many strengths and abilities that are often associated with autism. For example, many individuals with autism possess strong visual and spatial skills, which can be harnessed in a variety of fields, including art, architecture, and engineering. Additionally, many individuals with autism have strong attention to detail and a strong work ethic, which can be beneficial in fields such as finance, accounting, and information technology.

In conclusion, the inner voice of individuals with autism is an important and valuable contribution to society. By exploring the thoughts, feelings, and perspectives of individuals with autism, we can gain a greater understanding of their experiences and contributions, and work towards a more inclusive and accepting world. Through art, writing, advocacy, activism, self-help and support groups, individuals with autism are finding new and innovative ways to share their inner voice and build a more inclusive and understanding world for all.

Chapter 4.1: Presentation of the Thoughts, Feelings, and Perspectives of Individuals with Autism

In recent years, there has been a growing movement to give voice to the experiences of individuals with autism. Through personal narratives, advocacy efforts, and social media, individuals with autism are speaking out about their experiences and perspectives in a way that was previously not possible. This section of the book will present the thoughts, feelings, and perspectives of individuals with autism, offering a unique and important insight into their experiences and the challenges they face.

One of the most common experiences of individuals with autism is feeling misunderstood and marginalized. Many individuals with autism report feeling like they are living in a world that was not designed for them, where social cues, expectations, and norms can be confusing and overwhelming. They may feel like they are constantly trying to fit into a mold that does not match who they are, and that their differences are not valued or appreciated.

Despite these challenges, many individuals with autism also report feeling a strong sense of pride in who they are. They may feel that their unique perspectives and ways of looking at the world are a source of strength and joy. They may also feel a sense of connection with others who share their experiences, which can help to counteract feelings of isolation and loneliness.

It is important to note that these experiences are not universal, and that each individual with autism is unique. Some individuals with autism may experience intense feelings of anxiety or depression, while others may feel a sense of peace and contentment. There is no one right way to experience autism, and it is important to recognize and respect the diverse experiences of individuals with the condition.

One of the key experiences of individuals with autism is a heightened sense of awareness of their own emotions and feelings. Many individuals with autism report having an intense inner world, where they are constantly processing and evaluating their thoughts, feelings, and experiences. This heightened self-awareness can be both a blessing and a curse, as it can lead to feelings of anxiety and overwhelm, but it can also help individuals with autism to understand their experiences in a unique and insightful way.

Another common experience of individuals with autism is the struggle to communicate their thoughts and feelings to others. Many individuals with autism experience difficulty with verbal communication, and may find it hard to express themselves effectively. This can lead to feelings of frustration and isolation, as individuals with autism may feel like they are not understood or heard by others.

Despite these challenges, many individuals with autism report feeling a strong sense of creativity and imagination. They may feel like they have a unique and valuable perspective on the world, and that their experiences are worth sharing. They may also feel a deep connection to their passions and interests, which can be a source of joy and fulfillment.

It is important to remember that the experiences of individuals with autism are not limited to their diagnosis. They are individuals with a range of thoughts, feelings, and experiences, and they should be recognized and valued for who they are, not just for their autism. By sharing their perspectives and experiences, individuals with autism are helping to break down barriers and stereotypes, and to create a more inclusive and understanding world.

In conclusion, this section of the book presents the thoughts, feelings, and perspectives of individuals with autism, offering a unique and valuable insight into their experiences and challenges. By understanding the experiences of individuals with autism, we can help to build a more inclusive and understanding world that values and celebrates the diversity of human experience.

Chapter 4.2 Discussion of the Common Misconceptions and Stereotypes about Autism

The topic of autism has been surrounded by a multitude of misconceptions and stereotypes that have perpetuated a distorted and harmful understanding of the condition. These misconceptions not only harm individuals with autism, but also hinder the progress of society in recognizing the potential and unique qualities of individuals on the spectrum. In this section, we will explore some of the most persistent myths about autism and provide a more accurate and nuanced understanding of the condition.

One of the most persistent misconceptions about autism is that it is a mental illness or a developmental disorder that can be cured or treated with medication or therapy. This view is rooted in a medical model of autism that views individuals with autism as having something fundamentally wrong with them that needs to be fixed. This perspective not only disregards the complexity of autism as a neurodevelopmental condition, but also fails to recognize the strengths and abilities of individuals with autism.

Another common stereotype about autism is that individuals with autism are lacking in social skills and emotional intelligence. This stereotype is perpetuated by media depictions of autism as a condition that results in individuals being socially awkward, distant, and lacking in empathy. However, research has shown that individuals with autism have a wide range of social and emotional abilities, and that their difficulties in these areas often stem from a lack of understanding and support from their social and cultural environment.

Another harmful stereotype about autism is that individuals with autism are savant geniuses who have exceptional abilities in a single area, such as music, mathematics, or memory. This stereotype not only oversimplifies the complex nature of autism, but also places unrealistic expectations on individuals with autism and ignores the wide range of abilities and talents of individuals on the spectrum.

In reality, autism is a diverse and complex condition that affects individuals in different ways. There is no single "typical" individual with autism, and the strengths and abilities of individuals with autism vary widely. However, what individuals with autism share is a unique perspective on the world and a unique way of processing and experiencing information. This perspective and way of processing can result in difficulties in social and communication skills, but it can also result in unique talents, skills, and strengths that can contribute to the world in important ways.

To dispel the misconceptions and stereotypes about autism, it is essential to listen to the voices of individuals with autism and to gain a deeper understanding of their experiences and perspectives. In the next section, we will examine the unique strengths and abilities of individuals with autism and explore how their unique ways of experiencing and processing information can contribute to the world in important and valuable ways. By understanding the experiences of individuals with autism and recognizing the strengths and abilities of individuals on the spectrum, we can move towards a more inclusive and accepting world that celebrates the diversity of human experience.

Chapter 4.3 Examination of the Unique Strengths and Abilities of Individuals with Autism

In the world of autism, there is often a focus on what individuals with autism cannot do. This narrow-minded view ignores the numerous strengths and abilities that individuals with autism possess. This chapter will examine the unique strengths and abilities of individuals with autism and how they are contributing to society in meaningful ways.

One of the most commonly recognized strengths of individuals with autism is their attention to detail. They often have a heightened sense of detail, and this can be seen in their ability to notice and remember small details that others may overlook. This strength can be particularly beneficial in fields like science and technology, where precision and accuracy are essential.

Another strength of individuals with autism is their ability to focus on a single task for extended periods of time. This makes them excellent problem-solvers and can be invaluable in a variety of settings, including the workplace, where they can tackle complex projects with ease.

Individuals with autism are also known for their honesty and integrity. They are often highly ethical, and they do not engage in manipulative or deceitful behavior. This trait can be especially beneficial in careers like accounting or law, where honesty and integrity are essential.

Individuals with autism are also often creative and imaginative. They often have unique perspectives and ideas that can be very valuable in fields like art, music, and writing. For example, one individual with autism became a successful writer by using their vivid imagination to create captivating stories.

Finally, individuals with autism are known for their strong memory skills. They often have exceptional memories and can recall information that others may have forgotten. This can be particularly useful in fields like history and law, where a strong memory is essential.

It is important to recognize the strengths and abilities of individuals with autism, and to support and celebrate their contributions to society. By doing so, we can help to create a more inclusive and accepting world where individuals with autism are valued and respected.

In conclusion, this chapter has examined the unique strengths and abilities of individuals with autism and how they are contributing to society in meaningful ways. It is time to shift our focus from the limitations of autism to the numerous strengths and abilities of individuals with autism. By doing so, we can help to create a more inclusive and accepting world where individuals with autism are valued and respected.

Chapter 4.3.1 Creativity and Innovation in Autism

As we delve deeper into the inner world of autism, it is important to acknowledge the unique strengths and abilities that individuals with autism possess. One of the most notable areas of strength is creativity and innovation.

Individuals with autism often have exceptional abilities in areas such as art, music, and mathematics. They possess a keen eye for detail, a deep sense of logic, and a desire for precision. These skills are often demonstrated in their imaginative and innovative ideas and projects, which often challenge our perceptions of reality and the world around us.

For example, an individual with autism may create an elaborate sculpture made entirely from recycled materials. This work may be so detailed and intricate that it captivates the viewer's attention for hours, leaving them in awe of the artist's skill and creativity.

Similarly, an individual with autism may possess exceptional musical talent, performing complex pieces with ease and precision. Their musical ability may be so advanced that they can perform a piece after hearing it just once, and their performances often leave the audience stunned.

In the field of mathematics, individuals with autism are often able to perform complex calculations with ease and accuracy. They are able to see patterns and relationships that others may miss, and their ability to manipulate numbers is often unmatched. This can lead to their contribution to the development of new mathematical theories and concepts, which have the potential to impact our understanding of the world in a significant way.

In art, individuals with autism often have a unique perspective, producing works that are unlike anything seen before. They are able to express themselves in ways that are both deeply personal and universal, and their works often have the power to evoke strong emotions and provoke thought.

However, despite their exceptional abilities, individuals with autism often face barriers to fully expressing their creativity and innovations. Society may not understand their perspectives or value their contributions, and they may struggle to communicate their ideas effectively.

It is important that we recognize the unique strengths and abilities of individuals with autism, and that we work to create a world that values and supports their contributions. By doing so, we will be able to tap into the wealth of creativity and innovation that individuals with autism possess, and in doing so, we will help to make our world a better place.

In conclusion, individuals with autism possess exceptional abilities in areas such as art, music, mathematics, and innovation. These abilities often challenge our perceptions of reality and have the potential to make a significant impact on our world. It is our responsibility to support and empower individuals with autism to fully express their creativity and innovations, and to create a world that values and appreciates their contributions.

Chapter 4.3.2 The Importance of Self-Expression and Advocacy

The lives of individuals with autism can often be characterized by misunderstandings and negative stereotypes perpetuated by the wider society. The reality of their experiences, thoughts, and perspectives is much more complex and diverse, and their voice often goes unheard in public discourse. In this section, we will explore the importance of self-expression and advocacy in the lives of individuals with autism and the role they can play in shaping a more inclusive and accepting world.

Self-expression is the act of conveying one's thoughts, feelings, and perspectives in a manner that is authentic and true to oneself. It is a crucial aspect of mental health and well-being and allows individuals to connect with others, form meaningful relationships, and feel a sense of belonging. For individuals with autism, self-expression is especially important, as it can help to dispel harmful stereotypes and misconceptions about the condition and provide a platform for them to share their experiences.

One way in which individuals with autism can engage in self-expression is through creative pursuits, such as art, music, or writing. These activities provide a space for them to explore their thoughts and feelings and to connect with others who share similar experiences. The works produced by individuals with autism can be especially powerful and thought-provoking, as they offer a unique perspective on the world and challenge societal norms and expectations.

Another form of self-expression that is increasingly prevalent in the autism community is advocacy. Advocacy is the act of speaking up for oneself or others and advocating for the rights and needs of individuals with autism. It can take many forms, including online activism, speaking engagements, and participating in public policy discussions.

Advocacy is especially important for individuals with autism, as it provides a platform for them to share their experiences and raise awareness about the challenges they face. It also gives them a sense of agency and control over their lives, empowering them to shape the world around them in a way that is more inclusive and accepting.

One of the key benefits of advocacy is that it can help to dispel harmful stereotypes and misconceptions about autism. By speaking out about their experiences and perspectives, individuals with autism can challenge popular assumptions about the condition and demonstrate the diversity of the autism spectrum. This, in turn, can help to build greater understanding and acceptance of autism in the wider community.

Advocacy can also have practical implications for the lives of individuals with autism. By speaking up about their needs and rights, they can influence public policy and improve access to resources and support. For example, individuals with autism who are involved in advocacy efforts may push for greater access to housing, employment, and healthcare services that meet their unique needs and abilities.

In conclusion, self-expression and advocacy are crucial aspects of the lives of individuals with autism. By engaging in these activities, they can challenge harmful stereotypes, raise awareness about the experiences of autism, and shape a more inclusive and accepting world. It is our hope that by providing a platform for self-expression and advocacy, we can empower individuals with autism to tell their stories and to shape their own destinies.

Chapter 4.3.3 A Unique Perspective on the World

One of the most fascinating aspects of autism is the unique perspective that individuals on the spectrum bring to the world. Many individuals with autism have a highly specialized and intense focus on certain topics or areas of interest. This depth of knowledge and understanding can often lead to insights and contributions that are groundbreaking and highly valuable.

One of the most well-known individuals with autism is Temple Grandin, a professor of animal science at Colorado State University and a widely recognized expert in the field of animal behavior. Grandin has been open about her experiences growing up with autism, and has shared her perspective on how her autism has allowed her to have a unique and deep understanding of the way that animals think and behave.

Grandin's work has revolutionized the way that we think about animal welfare, and has been instrumental in improving the lives of millions of animals around the world. Her insights into animal behavior and her ability to translate this knowledge into practical solutions has earned her widespread recognition and respect within the field of animal science.

Another area where individuals with autism can bring a unique perspective is in the field of technology. Many individuals with autism are highly skilled at solving complex problems and developing innovative solutions. They may have a heightened ability to focus on and analyze complex systems and processes, making them ideal candidates for careers in fields such as computer programming, software development, and engineering.

In recent years, there has been growing recognition of the importance of neurodiversity in the tech industry, and many companies are now actively seeking out individuals with autism to work in their research and development departments. This trend is driven by the recognition that individuals with autism can bring a unique and valuable perspective to the problem-solving process, and can help to drive innovation in a range of areas, from artificial intelligence to cybersecurity.

Another area where individuals with autism can bring a unique perspective is in the field of art and design. Many individuals with autism are highly imaginative and creative, and have an eye for detail and precision that is unmatched. This combination of skills and talents can lead to truly original and groundbreaking works of art and design.

One such example is the artist and designer Timjah, who has autism and is known for his intricate and detailed drawings of animals and nature. Timjah's work is widely admired for its intricate patterns and precise lines, and has been featured in galleries and exhibitions around the world.

In conclusion, individuals with autism can bring a unique perspective to the world that is valuable and insightful. Whether it is in the field of animal behavior, technology, or art and design, individuals with autism are able to bring a new and innovative approach to problem-solving and to creating new and exciting works of art and design. It is important that we continue to support and nurture this neurodiversity, and to recognize the many strengths and abilities that individuals with autism bring to the world.

Chapter 5: Navigating the World with Autism

Living with autism can be a challenging experience, as individuals on the spectrum face unique obstacles in navigating the world around them. However, with the right support and resources, individuals with autism can lead fulfilling and successful lives. This chapter will explore the various support systems and resources available to individuals with autism, as well as the role of families, educators, and healthcare providers in supporting individuals with autism.

Overview of Support Systems and Resources

Individuals with autism require a range of support and resources in order to thrive. These support systems can include educational and therapeutic services, assistive technology, and community-based programs. The first step in accessing these resources is to receive a diagnosis of autism, which can be obtained through a multidisciplinary evaluation by healthcare professionals.

Once a diagnosis has been made, individuals with autism and their families can work with healthcare providers to develop an individualized support plan. This plan may include educational and therapeutic services, such as speech and occupational therapy, as well as assistive technology, such as communication devices. In addition, community-based programs can provide social and recreational opportunities, as well as opportunities for individuals with autism to develop their skills and independence.

Role of Families, Educators, and Healthcare Providers

Families, educators, and healthcare providers play a crucial role in supporting individuals with autism. Families are often the first line of support, providing a safe and supportive environment for individuals with autism to grow and develop. Educators can provide specialized educational services, such as early intervention programs and special education services, to help individuals with autism reach their full potential.

Healthcare providers can provide medical and therapeutic services, such as speech and occupational therapy, and can also collaborate with families and educators to develop an individualized support plan. They can also provide information and support for individuals with autism and their families, helping them to navigate the complex systems and processes that are involved in accessing resources and support.

Challenges and Obstacles in Accessing Resources

Despite the availability of support systems and resources, individuals with autism often face challenges in accessing them. These challenges can include a lack of access to healthcare providers, long waiting lists for services, and a lack of insurance coverage for services. In addition, many individuals with autism and their families face social stigma and discrimination, which can lead to feelings of isolation and marginalization.

In order to address these challenges, it is essential for individuals with autism and their families to have access to advocates and support networks. Advocates can help to navigate the complex systems and processes involved in accessing resources, as well as provide emotional support and guidance. Support networks can provide a sense of community and belonging for individuals with autism and their families, helping them to feel less isolated and more empowered to navigate the world with autism.

Conclusion

Navigating the world with autism can be a challenging experience, but with the right support and resources, individuals with autism can lead fulfilling and successful lives. Families, educators, and healthcare providers play a crucial role in supporting individuals with autism, and it is essential that they work together to develop an individualized support plan that meets the unique needs and abilities of each individual with autism. Despite the challenges and obstacles involved in accessing resources, with the right advocacy and support, individuals with autism can overcome these barriers and thrive in the world around them.

Chapter 5.1 Overview of the Various Support Systems and Resources Available to Individuals with Autism

Autism is a complex and multifaceted condition that affects individuals in a variety of ways. As a result, navigating the world with autism often requires a range of support systems and resources to help individuals with autism meet their needs and reach their full potential. In this chapter, we will examine the various support systems and resources available to individuals with autism, including education, therapy, and community-based programs.

One of the key support systems for individuals with autism is education. Many individuals with autism require specialized education to meet their unique needs and help them achieve their full potential. Special education programs for individuals with autism typically focus on teaching social, behavioral, and communication skills, as well as other life skills that are essential for success in the community. These programs may also incorporate occupational therapy, speech therapy, and other therapeutic interventions to help individuals with autism develop the skills they need to navigate the world.

Another important support system for individuals with autism is therapy. Many individuals with autism benefit from a variety of therapeutic interventions, including behavioral therapy, speech therapy, and occupational therapy. Behavioral therapy, for example, can help individuals with autism develop social skills, regulate their emotions, and manage their behavior in a more positive way. Speech therapy, on the other hand, can help individuals with autism develop their communication skills and improve their ability to express themselves. Occupational therapy can help individuals with autism develop fine motor skills, sensory processing skills, and other important life skills that are necessary for success in the community.

Community-based programs are also an important resource for individuals with autism. These programs can provide individuals with autism with opportunities to interact with peers, engage in activities, and learn new skills. Community-based programs can include recreational activities, social skills groups, and other programs that help individuals with autism develop the skills they need to succeed in the community.

In addition to these support systems and resources, individuals with autism may also benefit from assistive technology and other resources that can help them navigate the world more effectively. Assistive technology, for example, can help individuals with autism communicate more effectively, manage their behavior, and engage in activities that may otherwise be difficult for them.

In conclusion, the various support systems and resources available to individuals with autism play a critical role in helping these individuals navigate the world and reach their full potential. From education and therapy to community-based programs and assistive technology, these resources can help individuals with autism meet their needs and overcome the challenges they may face in their daily lives. Ultimately, it is important for individuals with autism to have access to these resources and support systems to help them lead fulfilling and meaningful lives.

Chapter 5.2: Discussion of the role of families, educators, and healthcare providers in supporting individuals with autism

Supporting individuals with autism is a crucial aspect of helping them lead fulfilling and productive lives. This task requires the efforts of many individuals and organizations, including families, educators, and healthcare providers. This chapter will examine the role of these groups in supporting individuals with autism and the impact they have on their lives.

Families are the first line of support for individuals with autism. Parents, siblings, and other family members play a critical role in helping individuals with autism to develop the skills and independence they need to thrive. They provide emotional support, help to identify and access resources, and advocate for the individual's needs and rights.

For many individuals with autism, families are also the main source of support for their daily needs. This may include assistance with basic tasks such as getting dressed, preparing meals, or using the restroom. Families also provide support with communication, socialization, and other areas of development that may be affected by autism.

Educators also play a critical role in supporting individuals with autism. Teachers, special education specialists, and other school staff provide educational and developmental support, help to build social skills, and provide opportunities for learning and growth. They also advocate for the individual's rights and needs, ensuring that they receive the support and accommodations they need to succeed.

Healthcare providers, such as doctors, therapists, and psychologists, provide medical and behavioral support for individuals with autism. They help to diagnose and treat conditions that may co-occur with autism, such as ADHD or anxiety, and provide therapy and counseling to help individuals with autism improve their social skills and emotional well-being. They also play a critical role in advocating for the individual's needs and rights and helping families access resources and support.

It is important to note that while these groups play distinct roles in supporting individuals with autism, their efforts must be coordinated to be most effective. A coordinated approach ensures that individuals receive the full range of support they need, from medical care to education and behavioral support. This helps to ensure that individuals with autism have access to the resources and support they need to reach their full potential.

In addition to these support systems, individuals with autism may also benefit from community-based organizations and support groups. These organizations provide a wide range of services, from recreational activities and social skills groups to advocacy and support services. They provide individuals with autism with a sense of community and help to build social connections, which can be especially important for individuals who may have limited opportunities to form relationships and engage in activities outside of the home.

Despite the important role of these support systems and organizations, many individuals with autism still face significant barriers to accessing the resources and support they need. This may include a lack of awareness of available resources, limited access to transportation, or limited funding for services.

However, despite these challenges, families, educators, and healthcare providers continue to play a critical role in supporting individuals with autism. Through their efforts, they help to ensure that individuals with autism have the support and resources they need to reach their full potential and lead fulfilling lives. By working together and advocating for the needs of individuals with autism, we can help to create a more inclusive and supportive world for those on the autism spectrum.

Chapter 5.3: Examination of the Challenges and Obstacles Faced by Individuals with Autism in Accessing Support Systems and Resources

For individuals with autism, accessing the support systems and resources they need to live fulfilling and productive lives can be a significant challenge. This can be due to a variety of reasons, including limited availability of resources, inadequate funding, lack of access to information and support, and societal stigma and prejudice.

One of the biggest obstacles faced by individuals with autism is limited availability of resources and support systems. Despite the growing recognition of autism as a neurodivergent condition, there is still a significant gap in terms of the resources and support systems that are available to individuals with autism. In many communities, there are simply not enough programs, services, and resources to meet the needs of all individuals with autism, which can make it difficult for them to access the support they need.

Another obstacle faced by individuals with autism is inadequate funding. Many of the programs and services that are designed to support individuals with autism are underfunded and struggling to provide adequate support. This can mean that resources are limited, waiting lists are long, and individuals with autism are unable to access the support they need.

A lack of access to information and support is another major obstacle faced by individuals with autism. While there is a growing amount of information and resources available online, it can be difficult for individuals with autism to navigate this information and find the support they need. Furthermore, many individuals with autism struggle to communicate their needs effectively, which can make it difficult for them to access the support they need.

Finally, societal stigma and prejudice can also be a major obstacle for individuals with autism. Despite the growing recognition of autism as a neurodivergent condition, many individuals with autism still face significant stigma and discrimination in society. This can make it difficult for them to access the support they need and can also lead to feelings of shame, isolation, and self-doubt.

It is clear that there is still a long way to go in terms of addressing the challenges and obstacles faced by individuals with autism in accessing support systems and resources. However, there are also many individuals, families, and organizations working to address these challenges and improve the lives of individuals with autism. By continuing to raise awareness of these issues and by working together to create more inclusive and supportive communities, we can help ensure that individuals with autism are able to access the resources and support they need to live happy, healthy, and fulfilling lives.

Chapter 5.3.1 Navigating the Complex Healthcare System

One of the biggest challenges faced by individuals with autism and their families is navigating the complex healthcare system. From obtaining a proper diagnosis to accessing the right support and treatment, the journey can be both frustrating and overwhelming.

For many individuals with autism, the first step in accessing support and treatment is obtaining a proper diagnosis. This can be a lengthy and often difficult process. Many individuals with autism face challenges in expressing their needs and symptoms, and healthcare providers may not have the necessary knowledge or understanding of autism to accurately diagnose it. In some cases, individuals with autism may be misdiagnosed with other conditions, such as ADHD or depression, leading to ineffective treatments and further difficulties.

Once an individual with autism has received a proper diagnosis, they may face challenges in accessing the right support and treatment. There are many different therapies and interventions available for individuals with autism, but the quality and availability of these services can vary greatly depending on where a person lives. In some areas, access to quality services may be limited, and individuals with autism and their families may have to travel long distances or navigate a complicated referral process to access the services they need.

Additionally, the cost of these services can be a major barrier for many families. Insurance coverage for autism-related services varies greatly depending on a person's insurance plan and state of residence, and many families face significant out-of-pocket expenses in order to access the services their loved one needs.

The complexity of the healthcare system can also make it difficult for individuals with autism and their families to advocate for themselves and their needs. Many individuals with autism face difficulties in communicating and expressing their needs, and they may be unsure of how to navigate the system and access the services they need. This can leave them feeling frustrated and overwhelmed, and they may not receive the support they need to reach their full potential.

In order to better support individuals with autism and their families, it is essential that healthcare providers and policymakers work to simplify the healthcare system and increase access to quality services. This may include improving the diagnostic process, increasing the availability of autism-specific services, and providing financial support for families who need to access these services. It is also important to provide individuals with autism and their families with the tools and resources they need to effectively advocate for themselves and their needs. This may include training on how to navigate the healthcare system, resources for communicating their needs and symptoms, and support for advocating for themselves within the system.

By working together to address these challenges, we can help individuals with autism and their families access the support and treatment they need to reach their full potential and lead fulfilling lives.

Chapter 5.3.2 The role of advocacy and self-advocacy

Navigating the world with autism can be a challenging and overwhelming experience, and accessing the support systems and resources that are available to individuals on the spectrum can be a complex and difficult process. The role of advocacy and self-advocacy is crucial in overcoming these challenges and ensuring that individuals with autism receive the support they need to live fulfilling and productive lives.

Advocacy is the act of speaking out on behalf of individuals with autism and working to promote their rights and interests. Advocacy can take many forms, including working to raise awareness about autism, promoting changes in legislation and policy, and advocating for greater access to resources and support systems.

Self-advocacy, on the other hand, refers to individuals with autism taking an active role in advocating for themselves. This can include speaking up about their needs and preferences, setting goals for themselves, and seeking out the resources and support they need to achieve those goals.

The importance of advocacy and self-advocacy cannot be overstated. The healthcare system, in particular, can be a complex and confusing landscape for individuals with autism and their families. Access to care can be hindered by lack of insurance coverage, long wait times for appointments, and a lack of providers who are trained and knowledgeable about autism.

Advocates can play a critical role in ensuring that individuals with autism have access to quality healthcare services. This includes working to educate healthcare providers about the unique needs and experiences of individuals with autism, advocating for insurance coverage for autism-related services, and working to increase the number of trained autism specialists.

Self-advocacy, too, can be an important tool for individuals with autism in navigating the healthcare system. This can include speaking up about their needs and preferences, asking questions and seeking information, and advocating for themselves when they feel they are not receiving the care they need.

Beyond the healthcare system, advocacy and self-advocacy can play a critical role in ensuring that individuals with autism have access to the resources and support they need in all areas of their lives. This includes access to education, employment, housing, and community resources.

Advocates can work to promote policies and practices that ensure individuals with autism have access to inclusive education and employment opportunities. This includes working to eliminate barriers to access, such as discrimination and lack of accommodations, and promoting training and support for educators and employers.

Self-advocacy, too, can be an important tool for individuals with autism in accessing education and employment opportunities. This can include speaking up about their strengths and preferences, seeking out accommodations, and advocating for themselves in the workplace.

Navigating the world with autism can be a challenging experience, but advocacy and self-advocacy can play a critical role in ensuring that individuals with autism have access to the resources and support they need to live fulfilling and productive lives. It is important that individuals with autism are encouraged and supported in their advocacy efforts, and that the broader community works to promote greater understanding and acceptance of neurological diversity.

Chapter 5.3.3 Building Meaningful Relationships and Connections

One of the most important aspects of life for individuals with autism is building meaningful relationships and connections with others. This can be a challenge, given the social and communication difficulties that many individuals on the spectrum face. However, with the right support, education, and resources, individuals with autism can learn to build and maintain relationships that bring them joy, comfort, and a sense of belonging.

One of the key factors in building meaningful relationships is understanding and embracing the strengths and abilities of individuals with autism. Many individuals on the spectrum have unique talents, interests, and perspectives that can enrich the lives of others and help build strong, meaningful relationships. For example, some individuals with autism have exceptional attention to detail, making them ideal for careers in fields such as engineering or science. Others have a deep appreciation for music or art, providing them with a valuable and unique contribution to the world.

In order to build meaningful relationships, it is also important for individuals with autism to develop social skills and communication strategies. Many individuals with autism struggle with social cues and communication, which can make it difficult to form meaningful relationships with others. However, with the help of educators, therapists, and support groups, individuals with autism can learn to understand and navigate social interactions, and develop the skills they need to build and maintain relationships with others.

Another key factor in building meaningful relationships is finding a supportive community. This can include family members, friends, peers, and other individuals with autism who can provide encouragement, support, and understanding. In many cases, individuals with autism can benefit from participating in support groups or joining autism-specific organizations, which can provide opportunities to connect with others and build meaningful relationships.

One of the most important ways to build meaningful relationships is to embrace the importance of self-advocacy. This means advocating for one's own needs and wants, and communicating effectively with others to build relationships that are truly meaningful and fulfilling. This can include learning to assert oneself in social situations, negotiating boundaries and expectations, and seeking out opportunities for personal growth and development.

In conclusion, building meaningful relationships and connections is a crucial aspect of life for individuals with autism, and one that requires support, education, and resources. With the right support and resources, individuals with autism can learn to understand and navigate social interactions, develop communication strategies, and find supportive communities that can provide the encouragement, understanding, and love that they need to build meaningful relationships and connections with others.

Chapter 6: Building a More Inclusive World

As we delve deeper into the experiences of individuals with autism and the challenges they face in accessing support systems and resources, it becomes increasingly clear that our society still has a long way to go in terms of creating a truly inclusive world for all. While progress has been made in recent years, the reality is that individuals with autism are still marginalized and often face barriers in accessing education, employment, and healthcare.

In this chapter, we will explore the various social and political movements working towards greater inclusion and acceptance of individuals with autism. We will discuss the strategies and tactics used by these movements, including advocacy, education, and media campaigns. And we will examine the progress that has been made and the work that remains to be done to create a world that truly values and celebrates neurological diversity.

One of the key strategies used by advocacy groups and organizations is public education and awareness campaigns. These campaigns are designed to raise awareness about autism and the challenges faced by individuals on the spectrum, and to combat the many misconceptions and stereotypes that still persist in our society. By educating the public, these campaigns aim to increase understanding, reduce stigma, and create a more inclusive environment for individuals with autism.

Advocacy groups and organizations also work to effect change through lobbying and advocacy efforts. This can involve working with policy makers and government officials to ensure that the needs and perspectives of individuals with autism are taken into account in the development of policies and laws. It can also involve working with schools, employers, and other organizations to create inclusive environments that allow individuals with autism to fully participate in society.

Self-advocacy is also a crucial component of building a more inclusive world for individuals with autism. This involves empowering individuals with autism to speak out about their experiences and to advocate for themselves. This can involve training and support to help individuals with autism develop the skills and confidence they need to effectively communicate their needs and perspectives.

Finally, building meaningful relationships and connections is a crucial component of creating a more inclusive world for individuals with autism. This involves creating opportunities for individuals with autism to connect with others and build a sense of community and belonging. This can involve social and recreational activities, support groups, and mentorship programs that bring individuals with autism together with others who share similar experiences and interests.

In conclusion, building a more inclusive world for individuals with autism is a complex and ongoing effort that requires the commitment and collaboration of many different groups and individuals. It requires education and awareness campaigns, advocacy and self-advocacy efforts, and the creation of opportunities for individuals with autism to connect and build meaningful relationships. But above all, it requires a commitment to valuing and celebrating neurological diversity, and a recognition that every individual with autism has something valuable and unique to offer to our world.

Chapter 6.1: Overview of the various social and political movements working towards greater inclusion and acceptance of individuals with autism

The journey towards greater inclusion and acceptance of individuals with autism has been a long and ongoing one, marked by the tireless efforts of numerous individuals, organizations, and movements. Over the years, these efforts have resulted in significant progress and progress, with greater public awareness, understanding, and support for individuals with autism and their families.

The autism rights movement, for example, has been at the forefront of the fight for greater acceptance and inclusion for individuals with autism. This movement seeks to challenge the notion that autism is inherently a disorder or disability and instead embraces autism as a neurodiverse condition. The autism rights movement has been instrumental in advocating for the rights of individuals with autism, from the right to equal access to education and healthcare to the right to self-determination and autonomy.

Another important movement in the fight for greater inclusion and acceptance of individuals with autism is the neurodiversity movement. This movement seeks to promote the recognition and appreciation of neurodiversity as a natural and valuable aspect of human diversity, just like cultural, racial, and sexual diversity. The neurodiversity movement also aims to challenge the pathologization and stigmatization of neurodiverse conditions like autism and to promote greater understanding and acceptance of neurodiversity.

There are also numerous organizations and advocacy groups working towards greater inclusion and acceptance of individuals with autism. These organizations offer a wide range of services and support, from educational and therapeutic programs to advocacy and legal assistance. Some of the most well-known organizations include the Autism Society of America, the Autism Science Foundation, and the Autism Self-Advocacy Network.

In addition to these social and political movements, there have been numerous media campaigns and public education initiatives aimed at raising awareness and understanding of autism. For example, the annual Autism Awareness Month in April is a time for people to come together to raise awareness, educate the public, and show support for individuals with autism and their families. Other campaigns and initiatives, such as World Autism Awareness Day, have also been instrumental in spreading awareness and understanding of autism to a global audience.

The progress made in recent years towards greater inclusion and acceptance of individuals with autism is truly inspiring, but there is still much work to be done. While public awareness and understanding of autism has increased, many individuals with autism still face significant barriers and challenges, from inadequate access to education and healthcare to social stigma and discrimination. However, with the continued efforts of the autism rights and neurodiversity movements, as well as the dedicated work of organizations, advocacy groups, and individuals, the future of autism inclusion and acceptance looks bright.

Chapter 6.2 Discussion of the Strategies and Tactics Used by These Movements, Including Advocacy, Education, and Media Campaigns

As the awareness and understanding of autism have grown over the years, so too have the social and political movements aimed at promoting greater inclusion and acceptance of individuals on the spectrum. These movements have employed a variety of strategies and tactics in their quest for a more inclusive world. In this chapter, we will examine the most common and effective methods used by these movements, including advocacy, education, and media campaigns.

Advocacy: One of the most important strategies used by autism advocacy organizations is to raise awareness and promote understanding of autism among the general public. These organizations often work with government agencies, schools, healthcare providers, and other organizations to advocate for better policies and services for individuals with autism and their families. They may also provide support, resources, and education to individuals on the spectrum and their families.

Education: Another critical component of these movements is education. Many advocacy organizations aim to educate the public about the realities of autism and help dispel common misconceptions and stereotypes. They may offer educational workshops, seminars, and training programs for healthcare providers, educators, and other professionals who work with individuals with autism. They may also provide educational resources and materials for individuals on the spectrum and their families.

Media Campaigns: Media campaigns are another important tool used by these movements to raise awareness and promote understanding of autism. These campaigns may include public service announcements, social media campaigns, and other forms of mass media. They often aim to change public perception and reduce stigma surrounding autism, while also promoting greater understanding and acceptance of individuals on the spectrum.

One well-known example of a media campaign aimed at promoting autism awareness is the annual "Light it up Blue" campaign, organized by the international advocacy organization Autism Speaks. This campaign invites individuals and organizations around the world to light up buildings and landmarks in blue in recognition of World Autism Awareness Day on April 2nd. The campaign aims to raise awareness and promote understanding of autism, while also showcasing the talents and abilities of individuals on the spectrum.

Another important tactic used by these movements is the use of personal stories and testimony. Individuals with autism and their families are often powerful voices in advocating for greater inclusion and acceptance. They share their experiences and perspectives on the challenges and barriers they face in navigating the world with autism. By sharing their stories, they help to humanize the experience of autism and promote greater understanding and empathy among the general public.

In conclusion, the social and political movements working towards greater inclusion and acceptance of individuals with autism have employed a variety of strategies and tactics in their quest for a more inclusive world. These efforts have been instrumental in increasing public awareness and understanding of autism, reducing stigma and discrimination, and advocating for better policies and services for individuals on the spectrum and their families. As these movements continue to grow and evolve, it is our hope that they will help to build a world that is more accepting, inclusive, and supportive of individuals with autism and all forms of neurological diversity.

Chapter 6.3 Examination of the Progress that has been Made and the Work that Remains to be Done

Over the past several decades, there has been a growing recognition of the need for greater inclusion and acceptance of individuals with autism. This has led to the development of various social and political movements aimed at improving the lives of those on the spectrum. These movements have made significant progress in advancing the rights and opportunities of individuals with autism, but there is still much work to be done to fully realize the goal of a more inclusive world.

One of the most notable achievements of the autism rights movement has been the increased visibility and recognition of autism. This has been driven by advocacy, education, and media campaigns that have sought to raise awareness about autism and dispel common misconceptions and stereotypes. This increased visibility has helped to reduce the stigma and discrimination faced by individuals with autism and has paved the way for greater understanding and acceptance.

Another important milestone in the movement for greater inclusion and acceptance of individuals with autism has been the passage of legislation aimed at improving the lives of those on the spectrum. For example, the Individuals with Disabilities Education Act (IDEA) provides funding to schools to support the education of students with disabilities, including those with autism. Similarly, the Americans with Disabilities Act (ADA) prohibits discrimination against individuals with disabilities in the workplace and in public spaces. These laws have helped to create a more supportive and inclusive environment for individuals with autism.

Despite these advances, there is still much work to be done to fully realize the goal of a more inclusive world for individuals with autism. For example, many individuals with autism still face barriers in accessing healthcare, education, and employment opportunities. Additionally, those on the spectrum often struggle to build meaningful relationships and connections with others, which can result in feelings of isolation and loneliness.

To address these ongoing challenges, it is essential that the work of the autism rights movement continues. This includes advocating for policies and programs that support the needs of individuals with autism, educating the public about the experiences of those on the spectrum, and raising awareness about the unique strengths and abilities of individuals with autism.

One important area for continued work is in the field of education. Many individuals with autism still face significant barriers in accessing quality education and support services. To address this, it is essential that schools are equipped with the resources and training necessary to support students with autism and that those on the spectrum are given opportunities to participate fully in the educational process.

Another key area for continued work is in the field of healthcare. Many individuals with autism struggle to access quality medical care, often due to a lack of understanding and knowledge among healthcare providers. To address this, it is important that healthcare providers receive training and education on autism, and that policies are put in place to ensure that those on the spectrum receive the care they need.

Finally, it is crucial that we continue to work towards building a more inclusive world for individuals with autism by fostering meaningful relationships and connections. This includes promoting opportunities for those on the spectrum to participate in social and recreational activities, and encouraging the development of supportive networks of friends and family members.

In conclusion, the work of the autism rights movement has made significant progress in advancing the rights and opportunities of individuals with autism, but there is still much work to be done. By continuing to advocate, educate, and raise awareness, we can create a world where individuals with autism are fully included, valued, and supported.

Chapter 6.3.1: The Role of Media Representation and Public Perception

In recent years, there has been an increased focus on the representation of individuals with autism in media and the impact that this representation has on public perception. The media can play a powerful role in shaping public opinion, and this is particularly true in the case of autism. Media representation can influence the way that individuals with autism are perceived by the public, and this can impact the way that they are treated and the resources that are made available to them.

One of the challenges that has arisen in media representation is the portrayal of individuals with autism as either savant geniuses or as disabled individuals who are unable to function in society. This narrow and limited representation does a disservice to the wide range of individuals with autism, who are diverse in their abilities, experiences, and perspectives. Moreover, this representation can perpetuate harmful stereotypes that create further barriers for individuals with autism in their daily lives.

The autism community has made significant progress in advocating for more accurate and diverse representation in media. For example, the Autism Self-Advocacy Network (ASAN) is a national organization that is dedicated to promoting the voices and perspectives of individuals with autism in the media. ASAN works to promote positive representation of autism by educating the media and collaborating with filmmakers, writers, and other creative professionals to promote autism-inclusive storytelling.

There has also been a recent increase in the representation of individuals with autism in media, including in popular TV shows, such as "The Good Doctor" and "Atypical", as well as in movies like "The Accountant." This increased representation has helped to shed light on the experiences and perspectives of individuals with autism and to challenge stereotypes.

However, there is still much work to be done in terms of media representation and public perception. It is important that we continue to advocate for accurate and diverse representation of individuals with autism in the media, in order to challenge stereotypes and promote greater understanding and acceptance of neurological diversity.

The impact of media representation and public perception goes beyond just representation in popular culture. It also has a significant impact on the public policies that affect individuals with autism and their families. For example, public perception can influence the level of funding that is provided for services and supports for individuals with autism, and it can also impact the way that individuals with autism are treated in educational and employment settings.

Therefore, it is important that we continue to work towards more accurate and diverse representation of individuals with autism in the media, in order to promote greater understanding and acceptance of neurological diversity and to improve the lives of individuals with autism and their families.

In conclusion, the role of media representation and public perception is an important one, as it can impact the way that individuals with autism are perceived and treated by society. Through continued advocacy and education, we can work towards a future where individuals with autism are valued for their unique strengths and abilities, and where they are fully included and accepted in all aspects of society.

Chapter 6.3.2 The Importance of Policy Change and Advocacy

Advocacy and policy change are two of the most important ways in which society can work towards greater inclusion and acceptance of individuals with autism. Through advocacy, individuals with autism and their families can raise their voices and share their experiences with the world, making their needs and concerns heard and understood by those in positions of power. Policy change, on the other hand, is the process of changing the laws and systems that govern our society, in order to create a more inclusive and equitable world for all.

There are many organizations and advocacy groups working to promote inclusion and acceptance of individuals with autism, including Autism Speaks, the Autistic Self Advocacy Network, and the Autism Society of America. These groups work to raise awareness about autism and its impact on individuals and families, and to promote the idea that individuals with autism should be seen as valuable and important members of society.

One of the most important ways in which advocacy and policy change can help individuals with autism is by improving access to resources and services. For many individuals with autism, the lack of access to quality education, healthcare, and other essential services can be a major barrier to leading a fulfilling and productive life. Through advocacy and policy change, individuals with autism can help ensure that these resources and services are available to everyone, regardless of their neurodiversity status.

Advocacy and policy change can also help reduce stigma and discrimination against individuals with autism. By raising awareness and educating the public about autism and the experiences of individuals with autism, advocacy groups can help change public perception and reduce the negative stereotypes that often accompany autism. This in turn can help create a more accepting and inclusive society for individuals with autism, where they are valued and respected for who they are.

One of the most important ways in which advocacy and policy change can be achieved is through education. By educating individuals, families, educators, and healthcare providers about autism and the experiences of individuals with autism, advocates can help create a more inclusive and understanding world. This education can take many forms, including training programs for educators and healthcare providers, educational campaigns and events, and public speaking engagements by individuals with autism and their families.

Another way in which advocacy and policy change can be achieved is through media representation. By promoting positive, accurate, and respectful portrayals of individuals with autism in the media, advocacy groups can help change public perception and reduce stigma. This can include promoting media coverage of individuals with autism, as well as working to change the way that autism is portrayed in movies, TV shows, and other forms of media.

Finally, advocacy and policy change can be achieved through the involvement of individuals with autism and their families in the political process. This can include participating in local and national advocacy campaigns, contacting elected officials to express their concerns and needs, and voting in elections. By using their voices and their votes, individuals with autism and their families can help ensure that the laws and systems that govern our society reflect their needs and priorities.

In conclusion, advocacy and policy change are essential components of creating a more inclusive and accepting world for individuals with autism. Through advocacy and policy change, individuals with autism and their families can help ensure that they have access to the resources and services they need to lead fulfilling and productive lives, reduce stigma and discrimination, and be valued and respected for who they are. By working together, we can create a more inclusive world for individuals with autism and help ensure that everyone is able to reach their full potential.

Chapter 6.3.3 The Potential for Greater Understanding and Acceptance of Neurological Diversity

Over the past few decades, there has been a growing recognition of the importance of promoting greater understanding and acceptance of individuals with autism and other neurological diversities. Through a combination of advocacy, education, and media campaigns, social and political movements have made significant progress in raising awareness about the experiences of individuals with autism and the need for increased support and resources.

One of the key strategies used by these movements has been to challenge the negative stereotypes and misconceptions about autism that still persist in many parts of society. Through a combination of personal stories and research-based evidence, advocates have sought to demonstrate that individuals with autism are not just "quirky" or "eccentric", but that they are full and complex human beings with a range of experiences, perspectives, and emotions.

Another important aspect of these advocacy efforts has been to highlight the strengths and abilities of individuals with autism, many of whom possess unique talents and abilities that are often overlooked by the broader public. This includes things like exceptional attention to detail, strong analytical skills, and an innate ability to see patterns and connections that others might miss.

Along with these awareness-raising efforts, social and political movements have also been working to promote policy change and improve access to resources for individuals with autism. This includes efforts to increase funding for research, to provide better training and support for healthcare providers, and to ensure that individuals with autism have access to appropriate educational and vocational opportunities.

There is also growing recognition of the importance of creating more inclusive communities where individuals with autism are able to participate and engage as full members of society. This includes initiatives to improve access to public transportation, to provide housing and work opportunities that are specifically designed for individuals with autism, and to promote greater understanding and acceptance of individuals with autism in workplaces, schools, and other public spaces.

Despite the significant progress that has been made, there is still much work to be done to ensure that individuals with autism have the support and resources they need to lead full and fulfilling lives. But as more and more people become aware of the experiences of individuals with autism, and as more organizations and communities work together to promote greater understanding and acceptance, there is reason to be hopeful that we can create a more inclusive and supportive world for all individuals on the autism spectrum.

The potential for greater understanding and acceptance of neurological diversity is rooted in the growing recognition that we are all more alike than we are different. By breaking down the barriers and stereotypes that have long separated individuals with autism from the rest of society, and by promoting a more inclusive and supportive environment, we can help to ensure that individuals with autism are able to fully participate in and contribute to the world around them.

Printed in Great Britain
by Amazon

Discover the hidden world of autism and explore the inner experiences of those on the spectrum in this compelling and informative book. Through the use of personal narratives, historical and social context, and current scientific research, this book provides a comprehensive look at the experiences of individuals with autism. From the definition and symptoms of autism, to the unique thoughts and feelings of those on the spectrum, this book sheds light on the challenges and barriers faced by individuals with autism and the important role of families, educators, and healthcare providers in supporting them. With a focus on the human experiences of individuals with autism and the need for greater understanding and acceptance of neurological diversity, this book is a must-read for anyone looking to gain a deeper understanding of this complex and fascinating topic.

ISBN 9798376857724

90000

9 798376 857724